I0191027

Radiating Light in a Dark World

I have come as light into the world so that whoever believes in me would not stay in darkness.
John 12:46 (NCV)

By: Monica S. Drake
Visionary of the **I AM Movement**

Visit us on Facebook:
www.facebook.com/theIAMempire
www.facebook.com/MonicaShaDrake

For more information contact:
Monica S. Drake ~ theIAMmovement@gmx.com
and on Facebook
www.facebook.com/theIAMempire
www.facebook.com/MonicaShaDrake

Radating Light in a Dark World

And He said to me, "My grace is sufficient for you, for My strength is made perfect in weakness." Therefore most gladly I will rather boast in my infirmities, that the power of Christ may rest upon me.

2 Corinthians 12:9 (NKJV)

Radiating Light in a Dark World

TABLE OF CONTENTS

DEDICATION

This collection is *ALL* to the Glory of the only true and living God – the Father, Jesus Christ the Son, and the Person of the Holy Spirit. Without you I am nothing.

But thanks be to God, which giveth us the victory through our Lord Jesus Christ.

1 Corinthians 15:57

Radiating Light in a Dark World

ACKNOWLEDGMENTS

So very thankful to my mother – Linda M. Drake – for your faith and your strength. For being there for your baby girl through the thick and the thin. To my little brother – Alfred Drake Jr. – thanks for using your talents to the Glory of God. To my Tuesday night prayer group family and Min. Herbert Simmons – *We are who we are individually because of who we are collectively.* Love you guys to life. There is no way I could share this gift of prayer with the world if you guys allowed me to be comfortable and not walk in the anointing and the authority God has placed on my life. To my other mother-Willie B. Robinson-so grateful for you encouraging me and pushing me. To everybody who said or ever thought I could or could not walk in the things God has trusted me with – Thank you !
To every reader, may you find light and life in this dark world through the Word of God.

FOR WE WRESTLE NOT AGAINST FLESH AND BLOOD,
BUT AGAINST PRINCIPALITIES, AGAINST POWERS,
AGAINST THE RULERS OF THE DARKNESS OF THIS
WORLD, AGAINST SPIRITUAL WICKEDNESS IN HIGH
PLACES.

EPHESIANS 6:12

SALVATION

The book of James 4:14 (NIV) gives us a perfect picture of how temporary the things around us are...*ᵇWhat is your life? You are a mist that appears for a little while and then vanishes.* Why base your future on temporal things, something that will pass away.

The Word of God also says in 2 Peter 3:9 that He does not desire for any of us to perish but that we all come to repentance. Have you really taken care of your business for eternity?

Take a moment and search your heart right there where you are. Have you given God your best or are you giving Him the leftovers?

I challenge you right now if you haven't given your life to Christ, why don't you take a moment to do just that. You don't have anything to lose but you will lose your soul if you don't give your life to Christ. Come on and don't put it off for tomorrow; it's not promised to you. All we have is right now. Don't let the glitz and the glam of this world fool you. This earth is not our home. Now take a minute and give your life to Christ.

Repeat this prayer:
> *Lord I thank You for Your Son Jesus.*
> *I believe that Jesus is Lord.*
> *I believe that He was crucified,*
> *that He suffered and died on my behalf.*
> *I believe that You*
> *O God resurrected Jesus from the dead.*

I thank You for Your love O God.
Now God I repent of and confess all of my sins before You.
Thank You for washing and cleansing me of all unrighteousness.
I surrender all to You O God.

That's it. You just gave your life to Christ. Give God a praise right where you are. I'm rejoicing with you and not only that, the angels are rejoicing over the soul that the enemy just lost…and that's your soul. The enemy no longer possesses your soul. Your Father is no longer the devil, but the only true and living God the Father possesses your soul.

Now… don't forget to offer this free gift of Salvation to your unsaved loved ones.

Introduction

In this dark world in which we live, there has been and always will be one constant-the Immutable, Unadulterated, Everlasting Word of God. There is no-thing or no one that is capable of withstanding the power and the Word of God. Moreover, we shouldn't just look to the Word when we're in trouble; instead the Word of God should be inscribed on the tables of our heart and become our guide to living.

Tell me something. Have you ever been in a dark room and turned on a light and the room remained dark? I would take a guess and say your answer is NO! The Word of God is light and it *will* bring light to the dark places of your life and the Word will shed light upon the evilness in this world. The darkness is the sin of this world and to go a step further, the darkness=the sin in *our* lives.

The Word of God is Truth and it is Alive. It changes lives. Don't read the Word if you don't desire change. I promise you in the Name of Jesus, if it doesn't change your situation or circumstance immediately, the Word of God *will* change you. The difference may not be recognized right away, but I can guarantee-rather you read the Word under a rock or on the mountain top-a part of you is dying and darkness must flee. There is a circumcision (a cutting away) that is taking place as we engulf ourselves in the scriptures.

Now, do not mishandle the Word and think it's just words on a page-*No way*! Every word, every letter, has power in *and* through it. This is why we can't view Christianity totally through the life living of man, rather first through what God has spoken in His Word. I myself have had to take the long way home concerning the previous statement. We have to know who God is for ourselves.

When you come to know who God is for yourself, you find out that He is in fact - I AM that I AM, ALL-POWERFUL, ALL-KNOWING, ALL in ALL…your EVERYTHING!

How do we know God? We have to know what He has spoken (in the Word) in order to get to know Him. You can rest assure that if you make the Word of God a part of your everyday language, He will deliver on His promises. If God doesn't perform that miracle or move in the area of your greatest need, then trust and believe that His grace is sufficient as He said in 1 Corinthians 12:9. It's not a matter of if He will do it; when and how is the question that most often plagues our minds. We have to believe that God has our best interest at heart and trust and believe in Him without wavering. He said in Romans 8:28 that *all* things work together for good for those who love Him.

To some this book may not look like or mean much, but to me this is my act of obedience. He (the Father) *spoke it* and I *did it*. This is the manifestation of the Word working through me to impact this evil world and to bring people to the Father. As you read through this book, I challenge you to read the scriptures out loud and then proceed with the prayers. I guarantee the Truth and the Light (the Word) will change your atmosphere. I have seen the Word work for myself. Wherever you are and whatever you are doing, the anointing can find you right where you are. In a bed of affliction, bound behind prison walls, in a state of hopelessness, depression…whatever state you may be in right now, the Holy Spirit can and will arrest you right where you are. I challenge you, right where you are as you read through the pages of this book and further more as you pick up the Bible, read the scriptures *out loud* and yes I meant to repeat myself. And then begin to pray *out loud*. It is so important in changing the atmosphere of your life, we you command things to be through the power of the spoken word.

Now watch the Holy Spirit shift things not only in your life, but the lives of those around you. Whatever you stand in need of, may you find comfort within the Word of God. There is nothing you can ever ask for or face, that can out-do God. He already took care of your life. He knew what you would face even before you were formed in your mother's womb. So don't think just because you have messed up and you feel so dirty and unworthy that God can't forgive you and cleanse your life. He can peel back layers and reach *down* to pick you *up*. He can transform your life. And even for those who think that God has forgotten about you, He heard your cry and even counted your tears. Know this that it's all about timing. And while you are waiting, ask Him what it is that you are suppose to be doing instead of whining about how bad you got it.

In this book you will find expressions and words of encouragement given to me by the Holy Spirit to fight through one of the toughest seasons in my life. The topics include:

- Faith
- God's Love
- Healing
- Hope
- Love
- Peace and
- the Tongue

My prayer for everyone that reads this book is:

> *Father God, I pray that You would bless every person as they will find comfort in knowing You are God and You have ALL power. Help them to know that there is nothing that can come against them that You don't already have authority over. Lord God strenghthen them now. Touch their mind, body, and soul. Bless their families Lord God. Bless their ministries. Help them O God to have a mind like Jesus. Stir up the gifts within them Father.*
> *And for those who don't already know You, I pray they will come to know you in the pardoning of their sins according*

to Romans 10:9-10. I thank You in advance for the souls that are gonna come to You as a result of this anointed book.

And finally, Lord teach these Your people how to wait on You with patience. Help them to bare fruits of the Spirit. Your Word declares that if we hope in You we will not be ashamed. Teach Your people how to lean not on riches, but to lean on You. Help them to work the process. Although some may even feel like giving up in this hour, I speak life and light. Darkness must go as the light comes forth in the Name of Jesus. Thank you for restoration Father. And because You have shown us what the thief (our enemy) has stolen and attempted to steal ALL shall be returned to us seven fold because he just got caught slippin. We thank you for it Lord God.

No weapon formed against these-Your people, no weapon formed against us- shall prosper. And every tongue which rises against them in judgment, you shall condemn.

I bless You, praise You, and give You honor Lord. It's in the Name of Jesus I pray...AMEN...AMEN...AMEN!!!

I want to challenge each of you to change the way you think of and view your present circumstances. God got you in this and He *will* get His Glory!

Love you so much people of God. Be blessed!!!

Faith: Now faith is the substance of things hoped for, the evidence of things not seen.

Hebrews 11:1

Habakkuk 2:4 – Behold, his soul which is lifted up is not upright in him: but the just shall live by his faith.

> *Matthew 6:30-34 – [30]Wherefore, if God so clothe the grass of the field, which today is, and tomorrow is cast into the oven, shall he not much more clothe you, O ye of little faith? [31]Therefore take no thought, saying, What shall we eat? Or, What shall we drink? Or, Wherewithal shall we be clothed? [32]For after all these things do the Gentiles seek: for your heavenly Father knoweth that ye have need of all these things. [33]But seek ye first the kingdom of God, and his righteousness; and all these things shall be added unto you. [34]Take therefore no thought (Do not worry) for the morrow: for the morrow shall take thought for the things of itself. Sufficient unto the day is the evil thereof.*

Matthew 9:22 – But Jesus turned him about, and when he saw her, he said, Daughter, be of good comfort; thy faith hath made thee whole. And the woman was made whole from that hour.

Matthew 9:29 – Then touched he their eyes, saying, According to your faith be it unto you.

Matthew 15:28 – Then Jesus answered and said unto her, O woman, great is thy faith: be it unto thee even as thou wilt. And her daughter was made whole (well) from that very hour.

Matthew 17:20 – And Jesus said unto them, Because of your unbelief: for verily I say unto you, if ye have faith as a grain of mustard seed, ye shall say unto this mountain, Remove hence to yonder place, and it shall remove; and nothing shall be impossible unto you.

Matthew 21:21-22 (NKJV)– [21] So Jesus answered and said to them, "Assuredly, I say to you, if you have faith and do not doubt, you will not only do what was done to the fig tree, but also if you say to this mountain, 'Be removed and be cast into the sea,' it will be done. [22] And whatever things you ask in prayer, believing, you will receive."

Mark 11:22 – And Jesus answering saith unto them, Have faith in God.

Mark 8:48 – And he said unto her, Daughter, be of good comfort: thy faith hath made thee whole (well); go in peace.

Luke 17:5 – And the apostles said unto the Lord, Increase our faith.

Luke 17:19 – And he said unto him, Arise, go thy way: thy faith hath made thee whole(well).

Luke 18:42 – And Jesus said unto him, Receive thy sight: thy faith hath saved thee.

Luke 22:31-32 – [31] And the Lord said, Simon, Simon, behold, Satan hath desired to have you, that he may sift you as wheat. [32] But I have prayed for thee, that thy faith fail not: and when thou art converted, strengthen thy brethren.

Romans 1:17 – For therein is the righteousness of God revealed from faith to faith: as it is written, The just shall live by faith.

Romans 5:1-2 – [1]Therefore being justified by faith, we have peace with God through our Lord Jesus Christ. [2]By whom also we have access by faith into this grace wherein we stand, and rejoice in hope of the glory of God.

Romans 10:8, 17 – [8] But what does it say? "The word is near you, in your mouth and in your heart"[a] (that is, the word of faith which we preach): [17]So then faith cometh by hearing, and hearing by the word of God.

Romans 12:3 – For I say, through the grace given unto me, to every man that is among you, not to think of himself more highly than he ought to think; but to think soberly, according as God hath dealt to every man the measure of faith.

1 Corinthians 2:5 – That your faith should not stand in the wisdom of men, but in the power of God.

Pray this prayer
Father I thank You for Your Word for You declare if I have faith and don't doubt, I can speak to the mountain, to be removed and it shall be done. Lord as I look at the mountains in my pathway, I believe in Your Word that you gave me power and authority to speak and it shall be done. So I speak to the mountains of negative cycles, self-sabotaging behaviors, lack, anger, bitterness, sickness, poverty, and every other thing the enemy has planted in my life…they shall be removed. No more will I be stagnant because of the threat of failure, for this mountain will be cast into the sea. I believe You and trust in You God. Thank You for moving on my behalf. Thank You for perfecting those things which concern me. Thank You for moving for Your Name sake. I love You for being my All in All. In Jesus Name I pray…AMEN…AMEN…AMEN!

Ask, and it shall be given you; seek, and ye shall find; knock, and it shall be opened.

Matthew 7:7

God's Love

Romans 8:37-39 – [37]Nay, in all these things we are more than conquerors through him that loved us. [38]For I am persuaded, that neither death, nor life, nor angels, nor principalities, nor powers, nor things present, nor things to come, [39]Nor height, nor depth, nor any other creature, shall be able to separate us from the love of God, which is in Christ Jesus our Lord.

John 3:16 – For God so loved the world, that he gave his only begotten Son, that whosoever believeth in him should not perish, but have everlasting life.

Romans 5:8 – But God commendeth (demonstrates) his love toward us, in that, while we were yet sinners, Christ died for us.

Galatians 2:20 – I am crucified with Christ: nevertheless I live; yet not I, but Christ liveth in me: and the life which I now live in the flesh I live by the faith of the Son of God, who loved me, and gave himself for me.

Ephesians 2:4-5 – But God, who is rich in mercy, for his great love wherewith he loved us, Even when we were dead in sins, hath quickened us together with Christ, (by grace ye are saved).

1 John 4:7-11 – [7]Beloved, let us love one another: for love is of God; and every one that loveth is born of God, and knoweth God. [8]He that loveth not knoweth not God; for God is love. [9]In this was manifested the love of God toward us, because that God sent his only begotten Son into the world, that we might live through him. [10]Herein is love, not that we loved God, but that he love us and sent his Son to be the propitiation for our sins. [11]Beloved, if God so loved us, we ought also to love one another.

Zephaniah 3:17 (NKJV) – The Lord your God in your midst,
The Mighty One, will save;
He will rejoice over you with gladness,
He will quiet you with His love,
He will rejoice over you with singing."

1 Peter 5:6-7 – [6]Humble yourselves therefore under the mighty hand of God, that he may exalt (raise you up) in due time. [7]Casting all your care upon him; for he careth for you. (NCV) [6]Be humble under God's powerful hand so he will lift you up when the right time comes. [7]Give all your worries to him, because he cares about you.

Psalms 86:15 – But thou, O Lord, art a God full of compassion, and gracious, longsuffering, and plenteous in mercy and truth.

1 John 3:1 – Behold, what manner of love the Father hath bestowed upon us, that we should be called the sons of God: therefore the world knoweth (recognizes) us not, because it knew (recognized) him not.

Deuteronomy 7:9 – Know therefore that the Lord thy God is God, the faithful God, which keepeth covenant and mercy with them that love him and keep his commandments to a thousand generations.

Jeremiah 29:11 – For I know the thoughts that I think toward you, saith the Lord, thoughts of peace, and not of evil, to give you an expected end (hope in your latter end).

Proverbs 8:17 – I love them that love me; and those that seek me early shall find me.

John 13:34-35 – *[34]A new commandment I give unto you, That ye love one another; as I have loved you that ye also love one another. [35]By this shall all men know that ye are my disciples, if ye have love one to another.*

Psalms 136:26 – *O give thanks unto the God of heaven: for his mercy endureth for ever.*

Romans 5:2-5 – ²*By whom also we have access by faith into this grace wherein we stand, and rejoice in hope of the glory of God.* ³*And not only so, but we glory in tribulations also: knowing that tribulation worketh patience;* ⁴*And patience, experience; and experience, hope:* ⁵*And hope maketh not ashamed; because the love of God is shed abroad in our hearts by the Holy Ghost which is given unto us.*

Pray this prayer:
Lord God I thank you for Your love. I thank You that You loved me even before I was formed in my mother's womb. Thank You for covering and keeping me when I was yet a sinner. And Father thank You for displaying Your love and affection through Your only begotten Son Jesus Christ who paid it all just for me. I love You God. I adore You Father. I bow before You in a position of worship. Thank You for never leaving me. Now God help me to show love toward my brothers and sisters that You have shown me Father. I owe you my all. I will forever give Your Name the praise, the honor, and the Glory. In Jesus Name I pray...AMEN!

Healing

> *Matthew 8:5-10, 13 – [5]And when Jesus was entered into Capernaum, there came unto him a centurion, beseeching him, [6]And saying, Lord, my servant lieth at home sick of the palsy (paralyzed), grievously tormented. [7]And Jesus saith unto him, I will come and heal him. [8]The centurion answered and said, Lord, I am not worthy that thou shouldest come under my roof: but speak the word only, and my servant shall be healed. [9]For I am a man under authority, having soldiers under me: and I say to this man, Go, and he goeth; and to another, Come, and he cometh; and to my servant, Do this, and he doeth it. [10]When Jesus heard it, he marveled, and said to them that followed, Verily I say unto you, I have not found so great faith, no not in Israel. [13]And Jesus said unto the centurion, Go thy way; and as thou hast believed, so be it unto thee. And his servant was healed in the selfsame hour.*

Romans 8: 11 – But if the Spirit of Him that raised up Jesus from the dead dwell in you, He that raised up Christ from the dead dwell in you, He that raised up Christ from the dead shall also quicken your mortal bodies by His Spirit that dwelleth in you.

Isaiah 58: 8 – Then shall thy light break forth as the morning, and thine health shall spring forth speedily: and thy righteousness shall go before thee; the glory of the LORD shall be thy reward.

Psalms 30:2 – O Lord my God, I cried unto thee, and thou hast healed me.

Exodus 15:26 – If thou wilt diligently hearken to the voice of the Lord thy God, and wilt do that which is right in his sight, and wilt give ear to his commandments, and keep all his statutes, I will put none of these diseases upon thee, which I have brought upon the Egyptians: for I am the LORD that healeth thee.

Exodus 23:25 – And ye shall serve the LORD your God, and he shall bless thy bread, and thy water; and I will take sickness away from the midst of thee.

> *2 Chronicles 7:14 – If my people, which are called by my name, shall humble themselves, and pray, and seek my face, and turn from their wicked ways; then will I hear from heaven, and will forgive their sin, and will heal their land.*

Numbers 23:19 – God is not a man, that he should lie; neither the son of man, that he should repent: hath he said, and shall he not do it? or hath he spoken, and shall he not make it good?

Deuteronomy 7:15 – And the LORD will take away from thee all sickness, and will put none of the evil (harmful) diseases of Egypt, which thou knowest, upon thee; but will lay them upon all them that hate thee.

3 John 1:2 – Beloved, I wish above all things that thou mayest prosper and be in health, even as thy soul prospereth.

> *Psalms 103:1-5 – ¹Bless the LORD, O my soul: and all that is within me, bless his holy name. ²Bless the Lord, O my soul, and forget not all his benefits: ³Who forgiveth all thine iniquities; who healeth all thy diseases; ⁴Who redeemeth thy life from destruction; who crowneth thee with lovingkindness and tender mercies; ⁵Who satisfieth thy mouth with good things; so that thy youth is renewed like the eagle's.*

Psalms 107:20 – He sent his word, and healed them, and delivered them from their destructions.

Proverbs 4:20-22 – ²⁰My son, attend to my words; incline thine ear unto my sayings. ²¹Let them not depart from thine eyes; keep them in the midst of thine heart. ²²For they are life unto those that find them, and health to all their flesh.

Hebrews 12:12-13 – [12]Wherefore lift up (strengthen) the hands which hang down, and the feeble (weak) knees; [13]And make straight paths for your feet, lest that which is lame be turned out of the way; but let it rather be healed.

Jeremiah 30:17 – For I will restore health unto thee, and I will heal thee of thy wounds, saith the LORD; because they called thee an Outcast, saying, This is Zion, whom no man seeketh after.

Jeremiah 33:6 – Behold, I will bring it health and cure, and I will cure them, and will reveal unto them the abundance of peace and truth.

Isaiah 53:4-5 – [4]Surely he hath borne our griefs, and carried our sorrows: yet we did esteem him stricken, smitten of God, and afflicted. [5]But he was wounded for our transgressions, he was bruised for our iniquities: the chastisement of our peace was upon him; and with his stripes we are healed.

Psalms 147:3 – He healeth the broken in heart, and bindeth up their wounds.

1 Peter 2:24 – Who his own self bare our sins in his own body on the tree, that we, being dead to sins, should live unto righteousness: by whose stripes ye were healed.

Deuteronomy 5:33 – Ye shall walk in all the ways which the LORD your God hath commanded you, that ye may live, and that it may be well with you, and that ye may prolong your days in the land which ye shall possess.

Job 37:23 – Touching the Almighty, we cannot find him out: he is excellent in power, and in judgment, and in plenty of justice: he will not afflict.

James 5:15-16 – [15]And the prayer of faith shall save the sick, and the Lord shall raise him up; and if he have committed sins, they shall be forgiven him. [16]Confess your faults one to another, and pray one for another, that ye may be healed. The effectual fervent prayer of a righteous man availeth much.

Pray this prayer:

It's in You I live, move, and have my being. So as I belong to You oh Lord, I expect You to heal me. I choose to believe the report of the Lord. I hear the diagnosis, but I still believe You O Lord. Every word of death spoken over me, I resist in the Name of Jesus. Every seed of fear and doubt planted by the adversary, we curse right now by the power given to us as believers in Christ Jesus. This body, this temple belongs to You Father. By the precious Blood of Jesus, I command my mind – my thoughts – to come into the alignment of Your will for my life. I command my heart, my soul, my spirit, my emotions to be healed O God. It all belongs to You. What the adversary has launched out against me to afflict me, won't work. The prayer of faith shall save me and you will resurrect me. I speak healing to every part of me O God. I give no place to the devil. I declare healing over my mind, body, & soul.

In the Name of Jesus I pray-as I walk in victory…AMEN…AMEN…AMEN!!!

7LIFT UP YOUR HEADS, O YOU GATES!

AND BE LIFTED UP, YOU EVERLASTING DOORS!

AND THE KING OF GLORY SHALL COME IN.

8 WHO IS THIS KING OF GLORY?

THE LORD STRONG AND MIGHTY,

THE LORD MIGHTY IN BATTLE.

9 LIFT UP YOUR HEADS, O YOU GATES!

LIFT UP, YOU EVERLASTING DOORS!

AND THE KING OF GLORY SHALL COME IN.

10 WHO IS THIS KING OF GLORY?

THE LORD OF HOSTS,

HE IS THE KING OF GLORY. SELAH

PSALMS 24:7-10

Hope

Romans 8:18 – For I reckon that the sufferings of this present time are not worthy to be compared with the glory which shall be revealed in us.

1 Thessalonians 5:8 – But let us, who are of the day, be sober, putting on the breastplate of faith and love; and for an helmet, the hope of salvation.

Psalms 16:9 – Therefore my heart is glad, and my glory rejoiceth: my flesh also shall rest in hope.

Ephesians 1:18 – The eyes of your understanding being enlightened; that ye may know what is the hope of his calling, and what the riches of the glory of his inheritance in the saints.

Ephesians 1:20 – According to my earnest expectation and my hope, that in nothing I shall be ashamed, but that with all boldness, as always so now also Christ shall be magnified in my body, whether it be by life, or by death.

Psalms 38:15 – For in thee, O Lord, do I hope: thou wilt hear, O Lord my God.

Psalms 16:9 – Therefore my heart is glad, and my glory rejoiceth: my flesh also shall rest in hope.

Colossians 1:5 – For the hope which is laid up for you in heaven, whereof ye heard before in the word of the truth of the gospel.

Psalms 22:9 – But thou art he that took me out of the womb: thou didst make me hope when I was upon my mother's breasts.

Psalms 31: 24 – Be of good courage, and he shall strengthen your heart, all ye that hope in the Lord.

2 Thessalonians 2:16-17 – [16]Now our Lord Jesus Christ himself, and God, even our Father, which hath loved us, and hath given us everlasting consolation and good hope through grace, [17]Comfort your hearts, and stablish you in every good word and work.

> *Psalms 33:18- 22* – [18]*Behold, the eye of the Lord is upon them that fear him, upon them that hope in his mercy.* [19]*To deliver their soul from death, and to keep them alive in famine.* [20]*Our soul waiteth for the LORD: he is our help and our shield.* [21]*For our heart shall rejoice in him, because we have trusted in his holy name.* [22]*Let thy mercy, O Lord, be upon us, according as we hope in thee.*

Psalms 42:11 – Why art thou cast down, O my soul? and why art thou disquieted within me? hope thou in God: for I shall yet praise him, who is the health (salvation) of my countenance, and my God.

Romans 12:12 – Rejoicing in hope; patient in tribulation; continuing instant in prayer.

Psalms 71:5-6 (NCV) – [5]Lord, you are my hope. Lord, I have trusted you since I was young. [6]I have depended on you since I was born; you helped me even on the day of my birth. I will always praise you.

Psalms 39:7 – And now, Lord, what wait I for? My hope is in thee.

Titus 2:13 – Looking for that blessed hope, and the glorious appearing of the great God and our Saviour Jesus Christ.

Psalms 71:14 – But I will hope continually, and will yet praise thee more and more.

1 Thessalonisans 1:3 – Remembering without ceasing your work of faith, and labour of love, and patience of hope in our Lord Jesus Christ, in the sight of God and our Father.

Psalms 147:11 – The LORD taketh pleasure in them that fear him, in those that hope in his mercy.

Titus 3:7 – That being justified (cleared of all guilt) by his grace, we should be made heirs according to the hope of eternal life.

Psalms 119:116 – Uphold me according unto thy word, that I may live: and let me not be ashamed of my hope.

Proverbs 10:28 – The hope of the righteous shall be gladness: but the expectation of the wicked shall perish.

Proverbs 13:12 – Hope deferred maketh the heart sick: but when the desire cometh, it is a tree of life. (NCV) It is sad not to get what you hoped for. But wishes that come true are like eating fruit from the tree of life.

Jeremiah 17:7 – Blessed is the man that trusteth in the Lord, and whose hope the Lord is.

Lamentations 3:22-26 – ²²It is of the Lord's mercies that we are not consumed, because his compassions fail not. ²³They are new every morning: great is thy faithfulness. ²⁴The Lord is my portion, saith my soul; therefore will I hope in him. ²⁵The Lord is good unto them that wait for him, to the soul that seeketh him. ²⁶It is good that a man should both hope and quietly wait for the salvation of the Lord.

Zechariah 9:12 – Turn you to the strong hold, ye prisoners of hope: even to day do I declare that I will render double unto thee.

> ***Romans 5:1-5*** – *¹Therefore being justified by faith, we have peace with God through our Lord Jesus Christ. ²By whom also we have access by faith into this grace wherein we stand, and rejoice in hope of the glory of God. ³And not only so, but we glory in tribulations also: knowing that tribulation worketh patience. ⁴And patience, experience; and experience, hope. ⁵And hope maketh not ashamed; because the love of God is shed abroad in our hearts by the Holy Ghost which is given unto us.*

Romans 8:24-25 – [24]For we are saved by hope: but hope that is seen is not hope: for what a man seeth, why doth he yet hope for? [25]But if we hope for that we see not, then do we with patience wait for it.

Hebrews 3:6 – But Christ as a son over his own house; whose house are we, if we hold fast the confidence and the rejoicing of the hope firm unto the end.

Romans 15:4, 13 – [4]For whatsoever things were written aforetime were written for our learning, that we through patience and comfort of the scriptures might have hope. [13]Now the God of hope fill you with all joy and peace in believing, that ye may abound in hope, through the power of the Holy Ghost.

Psalms 130:5 – I wait for the Lord, my soul doth wait, and his word do I hope.

Psalms 146:5 – Happy is he that hath the God of Jacob for his help, whose hope is in the Lord his God.

1 Peter 1:13 (NIV) – Therefore, with minds that are alert and fully sober, set your hope on the grace to be brought to you when Jesus Christ is revealed at his coming.

Pray this prayer:
Jesus Christ the hope of Glory, I surrender to You right now. I hope in You Lord. I can't see anything unless You show it to me O God. My dreams, goals, ambitions, is all in You. I stand on the wall, bombarding Heaven day and night waiting for You O God. You said You would perfect the things which concern me. As I stare difficulty and adversity in the face, I show them You Jesus. If You don't save me from this, I can't be saved. I'm crying out to You O God. The only True and Living God. I need You to move. I need You to move for me. I cast all my cares upon You. Hope in You will not make me ashamed but happy. Do it for Your Name sake O God. In the Name of Jesus I pray...AMEN...AMEN...AMEN!

[5]Trust in the Lord with all thine heart; and lean not unto thine own understanding. [6]In all thy ways acknowledge him, and he shall direct (make smooth or straight) thy paths.

Proverbs 3:5-6

Love

1 John 4:18 – There is no fear in love; but perfect love casteth out fear: because fear hath torment. He that feareth is not made perfect in love.

Jeremiah 31:3 – The LORD hath appeared of old unto me, saying, Yea, I have loved thee with an everlasting love: therefore with lovingkindness have I drawn thee.

1 John 3:16 – Hereby perceive we the love of God, because he laid down his life for us: and we ought to lay down our lives for the brethren.

> *Matthew 10:29-31 – ²⁹Are not two sparrows sold for a farthing(4 cents)? And one of them shall not fall on the ground without your Father. ³⁰But the very hairs of your head are all numbered. ³¹Fear ye not therefore, ye are of more value(worth) than many sparrows.*

Romans 5:5 – And hope maketh not ashamed; because the love of God is shed abroad in our hears by the Holy Ghost which is given unto us.

> *Romans 8:35, 38-39(NIV) –³⁵Who shall separate us from the love of Christ? Shall trouble or hardship or persecution or famine or nakedness or danger or sword? ³⁸For I am convinced that neither death nor life, neither angels nor demons, neither the present nor the future, nor any powers, ³⁹Neither height nor depth, nor anything else in all creation, will be able to separate us from the love of God that is in Christ Jesus our Lord.*

Luke 6:27 – But I say unto you which hear, Love your enemies, do good to them which hate you.

1 John 5:14-15 – ¹⁴And this is the confidence that we have in him, that, if we ask any thing according to his will, he heareth us: ¹⁵And if we know that he hear us, whatsoever we ask, we know that we have the petitions that we desired of him.

John 13:35 – By this shall all men know that ye are my disciples, if ye have love one to another.

Proverbs 10:12 – Hatred stirreth up strifes: but love covereth all sins.

Romans 13:10 – Love worketh no ill to his neighbor: therefore love is the fulfilling of the law.

Ephesians 3:19 – And to know the love of Christ, which passeth knowledge that ye might be filled with all the fullness of God.

Proverbs 15:17 – Better is a dinner of herbs where love is, than a stalled ox (fatted calf) and hatred therewith.

John 15:13 – Greater love hath no man than this, that a man lay down his life for his friends.

Pray this prayer:
Heavenly Father, where unforgiveness, hatred, envy, jealousy, and every unclean spirit has taken up residence, let it be driven out by love. Lord cleanse my heart, my spirit, and my mind of every drop of unforgiveness. Lord I forgive, I let go, I move on because You love me and You have forgiven me. I choose this day to turn the page beyond where I have allowed myself to be stuck. I choose this day to love the ones who have betrayed me, lied on me, fired the weapons in my direction and wanted me to fail. I choose this day to love my enemies. I love them God because You love them. Now God I ask that You replace the way I have chosen to love others with partiality of mind and heart, with the way You love. Help me to love people with unconditional love. Not in a judgmental way, but without limits. Holy Spirit, I yield my hateful, stubborn, rebellious ways to you. The partial love stops here. This day I began to love people in the way that my Father loves me. I worship You, I love You Abba Father. Thank You for loving me inspite of me.
It's in Jesus Name that I pray...AMEN...AMEN...AMEN!!!

[1]The Spirit of the Sovereign Lord is on me, because the Lord has anointed me to proclaim good news to the poor. He has sent me to bind up the brokenhearted, to proclaim freedom for the captive and release from darkness for the prisoners, [2]to proclaim the year of the Lord's favor and the day of vengeance of our God, to comfort all who mourn, [3]and provide for those who grieve in Zion - to bestow on them a crown of beauty instead of ashes, the oil of joy instead of mourning, and a garment of praise instead of a spirit of despair. They will be called oaks of righteousness, a planting of the Lord for the display of his splendor.

Isaiah 61:1-3 (NIV)

Peace

Philippians 4:6 – Be careful for nothing; but in every thing by prayer and supplication with thanksgiving let your requests be made known unto God.

1 Peter 5:7 – Casting all your care upon him; for he careth for you.

Romans 12:18 – If it be possible, as much as lieth in you, live peaceably with all men.

Isaiah 26:3 – Thou wilt keep him in perfect peace, whose mind is stayed on thee: because he trusteth in thee.

John 16:33 - These things I have spoken unto you, that in me ye might have peace. In the world ye shall have tribulation: but be of good cheer; I have overcome the world.

Philippians 4:9 (NIV) - Whatever you have learned or received or heard from me, or seen in me—put it into practice. And the God of peace will be with you.

Isaiah 12:2 - Behold, God is my salvation; I will trust, and not be afraid: for the LORD JEHOVAH is my strength and my song; he also is become my salvation.

Romans 15:13 - Now the God of hope fill you with all joy and peace in believing, that ye may abound in hope, through the power of the Holy Ghost.

Romans 8:6 - For to be carnally minded is death; but to be spiritually minded is life and peace.

1 Peter Chapter 3

⁹ Not rendering evil for evil, or railing for railing: but contrariwise blessing; knowing that ye are thereunto called, that ye should inherit a blessing.

[10] For he that will love life, and see good days, let him refrain his tongue from evil, and his lips that they speak no guile:

[11] Let him eschew evil, and do good; let him seek peace, and ensue it.

1 Corinthians 14:33 – For God is not the author of confusion, but of peace, as in all churches of the saints.

Isaiah 54:10 – For the mountains shall depart, and the hills be removed; but my kindness shall not depart from thee, neither shall the covenant of my peace be removed, saith the Lord that hath mercy on thee.

1 Peter 5:6-7 – [5]Humble yourselves therefore under the mighty hand of God, that he may exalt you in due time: [7]Casting all your care upon him; for he careth for you.

Philemon 1:3 – Grace to you, and peace, from God our Father and the Lord Jesus Christ.

Romans 14:17 – For the kingdom of God is not meat and drink; but righteousness, and peace, and joy in the Holy Ghost.

Psalms 119:127 – Therefore I love thy commandments above gold; yea, above fine gold.

1 Thessalonians 5:15 – See that none render evil for evil unto any man; but ever follow that which is good, both among yourselves, and to all men.

Colossians 3:15 – And let the peace of God rule in your hearts, to the which also ye are called in one body; and be ye thankful.

Proverbs 16:7 – When a man's ways please the LORD, he maketh even his enemies to be at peace with him.

Psalms 4:8 – I will both lay me down in peace, and sleep: for thou, LORD, only makest me dwell in safety.

James 3:18 – And the fruit of righteousness is sown in peace of them that make peace.

Psalms 37:4 – Delight thyself also in the LORD; and he shall give thee the desires of thine heart.

Proverbs 3:24 – When thou liest down, thou shalt not be afraid: yea, thou shalt lie down, and thy sleep shall be sweet.

John 7:38 – He that believeth on me, as the scripture hath said, out of his belly shall flow rivers of living water.

Psalms 34:14 – Depart from evil, and do good; seek peace, and pursue it.

Romans 5:1 – Therefore being justified by faith, we have peace with God through our Lord Jesus Christ:

Malachi 2:5 – My covenant was with him of life and peace; and I gave them to him for the fear wherewith he feared me, and was afraid before my name.

Jeremiah 33:6 – Behold, I will bring it health and cure, and I will cure them, and will reveal unto them the abundance of peace and truth.

Isaiah 55:12 – For ye shall go out with joy, and be led forth with peace: the mountains and the hills shall break forth before you into singing, and all the trees of the field shall clap their hands.

Isaiah 41:10 – Fear thou not; for I am with thee: be not dismayed; for I am thy God: I will strengthen thee; yea, I will help thee; yea, I will uphold thee with the right hand of my righteousness.

Haggai 2:9 – The glory of this latter house shall be greater than of the former, saith the LORD of hosts: and in this place will I give peace, saith the LORD of hosts.

Isaiah 53: 5 – But he was wounded for our transgressions, he was bruised for our iniquities: the chastisement of our peace was upon him; and with his stripes we are healed.

Pray this prayer:

Peace of God, O Spirit of the only true and living God...the peace that surpasses all understanding, I call on You to reign, rest, rule, and abide in my life. I need the Holy Spirit to stand up in me. Drive out all distress and anything contrary to the will of God. Every spirit of worry, fret, fear, doubt and any other spirit that's not of You O God, drive them out now in the Name of Jesus. I bind the enemy now and loose Your anointing in those areas where I have allowed the enemy space. I submit myself to You O God, resist the devil and he has to flee from me. I loose the blood, the water, and the Spirit over my mind, my spirit, every fiber of my being. Possess my soul O Lord. Thank You for Your peace O God. In the Name of Jesus I pray...AMEN!

the Tongue

What the book of Proverbs has to say...

c6v16-19 – [16]These six things doth the Lord hate: yea, seven are an abomination unto him: [17]A proud look, a lying tongue, and hands that shed innocent blood, [18]An heart that deviseth wicked imaginations, feet that be swift in running to mischief, [19]A false witness that speaketh lies, and he that soweth discord among brethren.

c10v19 – In the multitude of words there wanteth not sin: but he that refraineth his lips is wise.

c10v20 – The tongue of the just is as choice silver: the heart of the wicked is little worth.

c10v21 – The lips of the righteous feed many: but fools die for want of wisdom.

c10v31 – The mouth of the just bringeth forth wisdom: but the froward tongue shall be cut out.

c12v18 – There is that speaketh like the piercings of a sword: but the tongue of the wise is health.

c13v3 – He that keepeth his mouth keepeth his life: but he that openeth wide his lips shall have destruction.

c15v1 – A soft answer turneth away wrath: but grievous words stir up anger.

c15v2 – The tongue of the wise useth knowledge aright: but the mouth of fools poureth out foolishness.

c15v4 (NCV) – As a tree gives fruit, healing words give life, but dishonest words crush the spirit.

c15v23 (NIV)– A person finds joy in giving an apt reply—and how good is a timely word!

c15v28 – The heart of the righteous studieth to answer: but the mouth of the wicked poureth out evil things.

c17v4(NIV) – A wicked person listens to deceitful lips; a liar pays attention to a destructive tongue.

c17v20 (NCV)– A person with an evil heart will find no success, and the person whose words are evil will get into trouble.

c17v27 – He that hath knowledge spareth his words: and a man of understanding is of an excellent spirit.

c18v21 – Death and life are in the power of the tongue: and they that love it shall eat the fruit thereof.

c18v8 – The words of a talebearer are as wounds, and they go down into the innermost parts of the belly.

c20v19 – He that goeth about as a talebearer revealeth secrets: therefore meddle not with him that flattereth with his lips.

c21v6 (NCV)– Wealth that comes from telling lies vanishes like a mist and leads to death.

c21v23 – Whoso keepeth his mouth and his tongue keepeth his soul from troubles.

c28v23(NCV) – Those who correct others will later be liked more than those who give false praise.

c29v11 – A fool uttereth all his mind: but a wise man keepeth it in till afterwards.

c31v26 – She openeth her mouth with wisdom; and in her tongue is the law of kindness.

the Book of James…

c3v3-13 – ³Behold, we put bits in the horses' mouths, that they may obey us; and we turn about the whole body. ⁴Behold also the ships, which though they be so great, and are driven of fierce winds, yet are they turned about with a very small helm, whithersoever the governor (steerman will) listeth. ⁵Even so the tongue is a little member, and boasteth great things. Behold, how great a matter a little fire kindleth! ⁶And the tongue is a fire, a world of iniquity (sin): so is the tongue among our members, that it defileth (makes dirty) the whole body, and setteth on fire the course of nature; and it is set on fire of hell. ⁷For every kind of beasts, and of birds, and of serpents, and of things in the sea, is tamed, and hath been tamed of mankind: ⁸But the tongue can no man tame; it is an unruly evil, full of deadly poison. ⁹Therewith bless we God, even the Father; and therewith curse we men, which are made after the similitude (likeness) of God. ¹⁰Out of the same mouth proceedeth blessing and cursing. My brethren, these things ought not so to be (should not happen). ¹¹Doth a fountain send forth at the same place (opening) sweet water and bitter? ¹²Can the fig tree, my brethren, bear olive berries? Either a vine, figs? So can no fountain both yield salt water and fresh. ¹³Who is a wise man and endued (equipped) with knowledge among you? let him shew out of a good conversation his works with meekness of wisdom.

And the Word of God continues...

Psalms 34:13 (NCV) – You must not say evil things, and you must not tell lies.

Ephesians 4:29 – Let no corrupt communication (evil communication) proceed out of your mouth, but that which is good to the use of edifying, that it may minister grace unto the hearers.

Philippians 2:14 – Do all things without murmurings and disputing.

> *Matthew 12:33-37 – ³³Either make the tree good, and his fruit good; or else make the tree corrupt (bad), and his fruit corrupt: for the tree is known by his fruit. ³⁴ O generation of vipers, how can ye, being evil, speak good things? for out of the abundance of the heart the mouth speaketh. ³⁵A good man out of the(his) good treasure of the heart bringeth forth good things: and an evil man out of the evil treasure bringeth forth evil things. ³⁶But I say unto you, That every idle word that men shall speak, they shall give account thereof in the day of judgment. ³⁷ For by the words thou shall be justified, and by thy words thou shalt be condemned.*

Psalms 141:3 – Set a watch, O Lord, before my mouth; keep the door of my lips.

Matthew 15:11 – Not that which goeth into the mouth defileth a man; but that which cometh out of the mouth, this defileth a man.

Psalms 39:1 – I said, I will take heed to my ways, that I sin not with my tongue: I will keep my mouth with a bridle, while the wicked is before me.

Psalms 37:30 – The mouth of the righteous speaketh wisdom, and his tongue talketh of judgment.

Ecclesiastes 3:7 – A time to rend, and a time to sew; a time to keep silence, and a time to speak.

Psalms 119:171-173 – [171]My lips shall utter praise, when thou hast taught me thy statues. [172]My tongue shall speak of thy word: for all thy commandments are righteousness. [173]Let thine hand help me; for I have chosen thy precepts.

Pray this prayer:
Holy Spirit, sit on me and stand up in me. Kill everything inside of me that is contrary to the will and the ways of the Father. Cleanse my heart, O God. Your Word declares that out of the issues of the heart, the mouth speaks. So, Lord I ask that You would cleanse my heart, my mind, my body, and soul from all corruption. Help me to speak life and not death. Set a watch before my mouth and keep the door of my lips. Help me O Lord to be conscious and aware of what proceeds out of my mouth. I want to edify and exalt not tear down and murder with my tongue. Your Word says my tongue is like the pen of a ready writer. Help me to always be conscious that once words hit the atmosphere, I can't take it back. Lord I want to please you with everything. Now God, I ask you to use me to speak life into somebody else's life today. Use me to speak blessings that will change the pathway of destruction to the pathway of success in someone else's life. I am a vessel willing and ready to serve You O God. Anoint these lips and anoint this tongue. In the Name of Jesus I pray…AMEN…AMEN and AMEN!

About the Author...

Monica S. Drake is a servant of God who loves people. She is a Holy Ghost proclaimed W.O.G. (Woman of God). She found her inspiration and uncovered her gift of prayer when trouble came into her life as a result of her disobedience; yes the Holy Spirit said don't go down there and she thought it was the right thing to do. That's when she came to know the Heavenly Father beyond the form and fashion, but in a more intimate way.

In 2006, the Lord led her back to one of the churches she grew up in where-to this day-a prayer group meets every Tuesday night. Within this group of prayer warriors, God placed among them spiritual leaders who began to pull things out of her that the enemy wanted to keep covered. The enemy never really wanted her to see herself through the eyes of God. You see, it never was that she wasn't loved and accepted-and oh, yeah the enemy told her and she believed God didn't love her-but what she felt was the devil agonizing her because she impacted his kingdom and posed a threat to the kingdom of darkness. For most of her life, satan tormented her with self-confidence issues and a serious identity crisis. She couldn't understand why she was misunderstood and found it very difficult to fit in with the cliques. Through the prayer services, God began to show and speak into her who He created her to be. For the first time in her life, she began to recognize and understand the voice of God clearly and eventually found herself ministering to people through song and declaring what thus saith the Lord. Beneath the layers and after all of the pollution was filtered out, she saw who she was. During her personal devotion and group prayer services, her real character was formed and she began to hear her own language of prayer to the Father. As the Word began to impregnate her, she began to come up out of a position of pity and shame to that of a lioness-bold, fearless, tenacious, committed, and walking in love.

Fast forward now to 2013, after many trials, tribulations, and pain that seemed unbearable at times, oh and a very dysfunctional marriage later, well I mean two marriages later, she is still standing. The mandate over her life hasn't been clearer after the numerous testimonies of others and the confirmation God has brought as the result of prayer. Though she doesn't know where the next step will take her, she does have FAITH and TRUST that God will not lead her wrong. Time and time again, she asks, "God, don't you see my issues and the stuff that I do? How can you still choose to use me?" The fact that she knows who she really is, let's her further know that it is only God who has done this. No man can get the glory for the evidence of greater works-the thing you read now and 'shall be' that is to come. Just a few years ago, during a season of a struggle with self-confidence, in that same Tuesday night prayer service at Gould Branch Baptist Church in that very small community in southeast Georgia, the Holy Spirit gave her three words, 'IT SHALL BE!' On that very same night, I bet she had no idea that one of the things to come forth and to resurrect that night is/was this very same collection. And I can hear her say again, "Yeah this may look and seem small to some, but this is my act of obedience. And believe me after the mess that I settled for in my life that was far beneath me, this act is a cause for prayer, praise, and worship."

She is a humbled, virtuous woman who is a worship singer, songwriter, prayer warrior, and a psychologist in the making…oh and now an author (HALLEJUAH!!!)– look at God making way for her at the front of the line.

During a season of chastisement, change, and transition, the Holy Spirit spoke to her in a voice of authority, requiring that this collection be brought together in a plea of urgency to the Glory of God.

Not that she is self-proclaimed; instead she is Heaven-proclaimed. She believes that this is only the beginning and there are things inside of her that the world needs to hear.

Ms. Drake also wanted us to mention something to you all…the I AM Movement! You have to visit the Facebook page for more information. It's a vision God gave Monica just about 6 years ago and the pieces are still being put together, but it's all about shaping your world by speaking the Word of God and proclaiming some things to be in your life spiritually. And in the natural, it's a confidence builder. Knowing that you can do anything that you put your mind to without the confirmation and the acceptance of others. Silence the voice of the haters by continuing to speak life. Take hold of the hand of God and let's walk in victory and success.

For those of you who know the Word of prayer, we-the I AM Movement – we solicit your prayers. God has placed a burden on us for the souls. He is commanding us to minster to the young people. He is coming back ya'll. So look out, we are coming to a city near you. And remember we can't do this individually, but there is power and authority in numbers.

Jesus told us in Luke 14:23 Go out into the highways and hedges, and compel (urge) them to come in, that my house may be filled. Believe us we are going to do just that.

Love you all. God bless. xoxoxo

I have a question for you before you close this book…
Can YOU still give God praise through your pain….? As for
me…I can, I am, and I will continue to do so because He is there to
bring me *and* you through it all.

Sign,

Monica S. Drake

www.ingramcontent.com/pod-product-compliance
Lightning Source LLC
Chambersburg PA
CBHW071743020426
42331CB00008B/2157